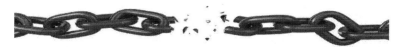

FROM
STRUGGLE TO STRENGTH

MARQUITA NESBITT

ISBN: 9798691633140

Red Pen Edits and Consulting, LLC

DEDICATIONS

This book is dedicated to every woman that suffers in silence. Understand that you have a voice and you don't have to settle for a relationship that is laced with domestic violence. It is my prayer that this book serves as a chronicle of a person's life that realizes their self-worth and value as they pursue freedom and fulfillment in every area. This book is dedicated to your testimony and success story of moving *From Struggle To Strength*.

ACKNOWLEDGEMENTS

I am eternally grateful to God for sparing my life in time to be a living testimony of His grace and sufficiency and for giving me the courage to finally tell my story.

To My Sons, Kenneth and Isaiah

I hope that you will grow into the mighty men of God that He wants you to be. Thank you for being Mommy's SONshine. You guys fought to live from day one and have been fighting ever since. Thank you both for loving me through it all. You've seen me at my lowest and motivated me without ever saying a word. You both have changed my life dramatically and I am forever grateful. I love you both with everything in me.

To My Family

To my biological mother, Missy - Thank you for showing me how to hustle and provide for my kids by any means. To my bonus mom, Romona – Thank you for your prayers and encouraging conversations. **I LOVE YOU BOTH!**

To my daddy, THE Carluse Baird – Thank you for loving and spoiling me! I am now and forever will be a Daddy's Girl. I love you old man! To my bonus dad, Richard McCoy Jr - Continue to Rest In Peace.

To my sisters, Marissa and Cyesha, and all of my brothers, Mike, Darvin, Rod and Marell - Thanks for being the best siblings ever!!

Lastly, but certainly not the least, to my God sister, Jill Banks - I appreciate you for being my way out. God used you as a lifeline to rescue me from situations wherein I couldn't save myself.

To Pastor Nate' and Lady Tarsha Jefferson – Thank you for instilling in the necessity of prayer and posture of what a Holy woman looks like.

TABLE OF CONTENTS

CHAPTER 1
PICTURE PERFECT

pic-ture
(noun) - *visual representation such as a drawing, painting, or photograph*
(verb) - *to imagine in your mind; to visualize*

per-fect
(adjective) - *beyond improvement, having nothing wrong*
(verb) - *to improve, to make better*

When you hear the word "picture perfect", what immediately comes to mind? What happens when you put the two definitions together? You have this visual representation of what appears to have absolutely nothing wrong. Well, that's how my love story began. I met this guy in college. He was the football star that every girl wanted. He was extremely popular at that time. I counted myself lucky to be the one he chose to date. He would walk me to class, carry my books, and purchase me food (when I refused to eat in the cafeteria). He even joined the gospel choir to spend more time with me. I was so in love with this man. Everything was perfect, or so I thought. Even in the beginning, there were warning signs - signs I chose to overlook. From the outside looking in, this was the ideal relationship. The star athlete and some country girl that showed up from nowhere. During the summer break, we were in constant communication with each other. Calling, texting, staying on the phone all night until early mornings was our normalcy. Then, he decided to relocate to my hometown. That's a day that I will never forget. We were at a church function when I got his phone call. I thought it was a prank. I asked him to describe his surroundings and sure enough, he was in Asheville. I went and grabbed my sister. I asked her to please take me to the bus station to get him. YES! I said it! - The bus station! Neither one of us were driving at the time. I thought that catching the bus to be with me was the sweetest display of affection. Once he moved to Asheville, I thought that all my worries were gone. My forever was in reach. I just knew that marriage was the goal.

My parents, however, weren't happy at all. First and foremost, because this relationship was not discussed with them. Secondly, shacking up was not an option based on how I was raised. Living together was a "no-no". Nothing or no one could tell me anything different. Finally, my parents allowed him to move in with us. While we were living with my parents, there were rules. No sleeping together was at the top of the list. He had an amazing relationship with most of my siblings, but not my sister. He was extremely helpful around the house. He helped with dishes and cleaning. He even helped my mom wrap the pipes under the house when they had frozen and burst. We finally decided to get our own apartment when space and conditions at my parents' house started to get tight. Life was good. We were living the ideal life. We had become D.I.N.K's (Double Income No Kids). We couldn't get enough of each other. When you saw one, you saw the other. We were a young couple that was simply in love. I wanted for absolutely nothing. I lived such a lavish lifestyle.

With him being new to the area, he had no friends. I thought it would be nice to introduce him to some of the guys who lived in the neighborhood. When he made new friends, he started drinking, smoking and hanging out all hours of the night. He started going to bars and clubs. This wasn't the guy I met and had fallen in love with. He was changing right before my eyes and none of it was for the better. More and more he was hanging out and spending less time at work and at home. The arguments started. The accusations started and the man I thought I knew, was no more. I started to question myself. Why did I introduce him to this group of people? Who was this man? Is this the man who said he loved me? He no longer wanted to live in the place we called home. He found another apartment closer to his new friends. Even in the midst of this initial chaos, I trusted him. Without second guessing, I politely packed my things and we moved......together. And then it begins.......

MY THOUGHTS

CHAPTER 2
THE TRANSITION

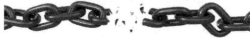

tran-si-tion
(noun) - *going from one state of action or position to another*

New things.
New people.
New environment.
New surroundings.

As I started to adjust to this new way of living, I must say, at first, things were good. We were closer than ever. We were bonding and hanging out. All was well. Then, things started changing. It wasn't anything that happened over night but you could definitely see the signs. I believe progressively worse can best describe this transition. The new friends that he made became more important than me. We would spend less and less time together. It had gotten so bad, that there were days that we would never see each other. The days of hanging out, watching movies, shopping, and simply enjoying each other were fading away. The tender love and heartfelt affection that I was accustomed to vanished into thin air. Then, I got pregnant.

I waited to tell him about the pregnancy. Ironically, when I told him about the pregnancy, things were starting to progress in the right direction. He was spending more time at home. We were back to a good place. Then, as time progressed, he would get aggravated at the thought of having to be in the house. Then, my presence was an issue. The arguments started and so did the belittling. I found myself dealing with depression and I eventually miscarried with my daughter in 2003. Battling depression alone is the worst feeling in the world. After some time, I gained my self-esteem and began to build myself up. Then, infidelity made an appearance.

There was a woman who lived in the same apartment complex as us in the next building. He started spending time with her. He was always at her house. They were hosting kickbacks, gatherings, playing spades, and drinking. For whatever reason, I was not allowed to attend. Doesn't that seem strange? Yes. You heard me right. I was not allowed to attend. The friends that I introduced him to, didn't want me around. Furthermore, my boyfriend didn't allow me to hang with them anymore. Then, I missed my cycle. Here we go again! This was a difficult time for me. I was just trying to get over a miscarriage and now I'm expecting another baby. The relationship was getting worse. One Sunday, while having dinner, I told him the presumably good news. His response was different and very nonchalant. I blamed the loss of our first child on him. I made a doctor's appointment to make sure I was pregnant this time and I went alone. His excuse was that he was too tired from the night before.

As time progressed in this pregnancy, I became more and more miserable. Things were happening and I felt like I had no control because I was pregnant. The levels of infidelity and confusion started to unravel. I started babysitting for one of his women. I would watch her son while they went out or while she worked. As time passed, more and more women came forward with information. One night, I watched two women fighting outside my apartment. Here's the thing – they were fighting over my man and I didn't know it until the next day. How humiliating!

By now, I guess you are thinking, "Why girl? Why?". Trust me! There's more. I would never forget our first real encounter. We had an argument about my location. He had been drinking so nothing that I said was right. I decided to leave. I was sitting in my car in the driveway at a friend's house just to get away and clear my head. That's when I heard him pull up. I immediately began to panic. Unsure of his actions, I tensed up. I didn't know what was about to happen. When he got out of his car, I was too afraid to look over. My anxiety was high and my adrenaline was rushing. While he's yelling to the top of his lungs, I blacked out and I hear nothing. The next thing that I remembered was the shatter of my car's window. This guy kicked my window in on the passenger side and then proceeds to pulls me out of the driver's seat. At this point, I'm in complete shock. I'm afraid to fight back. This began my life of living in fear. After that incident and much aligned with the cycles of domestic violence, he showered me with gifts and apologized for lashing out. He uttered the empty promise that it wouldn't happen again. Silly me, I believed him. This was the first time that he ever exerted physical contact on this level so I was easily forgiving of his actions. I started living my life walking on eggshells. I was overly mindful of my actions. I lived in fear of the unknown because at this point, anything could set him off. Abuse in multiple forms seemed to progress. Small arguments led to bigger arguments. Even with all of these calamities, I was still in love with a man that completely scared me.

MY THOUGHTS

_____
_____
_____
_____
_____
_____
_____
_____
_____
_____
_____
_____
_____
_____
_____
_____
_____
_____
_____
_____
_____
_____
_____
_____

CHAPTER 3
TRUST YOUR GUT

in-tu-i-tion
(noun) - *instinctive knowledge or feeling*

Have you ever had that gut feeling that something just isn't right? Have you ever had the urge to do something that you feel is out of the norm but it leads you to where you need to be to see something that you wouldn't have seen unless you went with your gut in the first place? Well, in this relationship of cycles and transitions, that was happening to me a lot. I would have these strange feelings at random moments that I didn't quite understand. Some call it "women's intuition". Women's intuition is an inept, embedded ability to feel or know something in advance of realization. It wasn't until I was out of the situation that I was able to fully understand. The warning signs were always there. I was just head over heels in love and I chose to overlook the signs. I have always been a home body. When I would leave the house, I felt that my boyfriend was exhibiting care for me by calling and asking about my whereabouts and how long I would be before coming home. Nope! It was the complete opposite. If he didn't know where I was, or who I was with, it was an issue. He allowed me to go to certain places such as work, church, and my mother's house. You know, the normal places. He just had to be aware of my location at all times.

There were times when he would want to know where I was so that he would have enough time to get the "other woman" out before I got home. Even if they weren't at our house, he would still have enough time to get home before I did since one of the women he was sleeping with lived nearby. My keys always seemed to get lost at the same time that he would go out. That way, I was stuck at the house.

One day, he took me to purchase a car because I was about to have his child and it was not suitable for me to ride around in a car with a busted window. I didn't want the car that he chose for me. That started another huge fight. I was deemed ungrateful, unappreciative, and a host of more degrading terms. To my surprise, when I pulled up in the neighborhood, there was the car.... that I did not want. I'm thinking to myself, there is no way this man bought that car. In actuality, because I didn't want the car, he took "his friend", the other woman, to get it. I was LIVID! How dare you take her to get the car that you wanted for me? Out of anger, rage and humiliation, I took a baseball bat that was in the house and proceeded to bust out every window on his new car. It felt good at the moment but overall, it was an awful idea.

He was in control of everything, including me. He would give me money to stay away from him. When he went grocery shopping, he would have someone to come sit with me so that I wouldn't be home alone. RIGHT!! He found me a friend. I suggested that my best friend move in since he was never here and he agreed. I was somewhat at peace. My best friend was there providing me with someone to talk to. I became a robot. I cooked. I cleaned. I had sex when he wanted and I stayed home. My life had become a miserable routine. There was no excitement. I was sleeping alone in an apartment that felt more like a prison than a home. I experienced mental torment with the continuation of emotional and verbal abuse. My best friend left because she couldn't deal with how I was being treated. One would think that I would've followed huh? No. I stayed where I was comfortable and where my dysfunction was highly functional. His controlling behavior had become my new normal. I felt so alone. I experienced my pregnancy alone while being stressed out and emotionally drained. Six months into my pregnancy, while lying in bed, alone and in pain (mentally and physically), I began to have contractions.

One night that I can remember so vividly, I prayed, "Lord, please let me make it thru the night" and I drifted off to sleep. I was awakened by an extreme pain. I looked around and he was not home. I get out of bed, walk to the bathroom and fall to my knees. I begged God, "please protect my baby!". I slowly stand up with fluid and blood leaking everywhere. I get up enough strength to walk downstairs, down the sidewalk while cramping and bleeding. I knock on the other woman's door. She answers. I replied, "can you please let him know, I need to go to the hospital?" He says, "I'm coming". I stand waiting, embarrassed, sick, and hurting. He takes me to the hospital and waits until I get assigned a room. Then, he leaves.

MY THOUGHTS

CHAPTER 4
PREMATURE BIRTH

pre-ma-ture
(adjective) - *something that's not fully developed; too early*

The date is February 6, 2004 and I have been admitted into the hospital due to a leak of my amniotic sac. I'm terrified. The doctor comes in and he proceeds to tell me that I will be on bed rest until my due date of May 26th. Like, are you kidding me? Bed rest for 3 months?! This can't be right. I begged the Dr. to allow me to go home to rest for the next 3 months even though those circumstances weren't favorable either. The answer was an unwavering "no".

Six days into my bed rest sentence, my situation wasn't getting any better. The pain is getting worse and as always, I'm alone. I'm calling the father of my unborn child and as always, he's busy but assured me that he would come by when he can. About 11pm of that same night, I started to feel more pressure and the nurses and doctors have become more frantic. There is so much going on so fast. Nurses made many phone calls and pages. I heard one of the nurses say, "Prep the room. We're going to have to do an emergency C-section." And then, the room stood still. My thoughts began to run wild. Is this the end for me and my baby? As I was being rolled out the room to go into surgery, I see my boyfriend in the hallway. He was going off! He was wondering why there was so much blood and losing so much blood. He was scared. In that moment, I needed him cool, calm, and collected and he was none of that. He asked my aunt to go into the delivery room with me because he couldn't stand to see me like that.

So, here I am, lying there in the operating room without the father of my unborn child. How could you miss the birth of your first born? Through it all, my baby was born. He was so small and tiny as ever - 1lb 9oz and 12 inches long. I never got to hold or touch my baby but I remember the tiny sound of his cry. From that time to now, I made a promise to always protect him, even if it was from his daddy. My son was transported to NICU where he would continue to grow. Once in recovery, the doctors came in to give me an update on what I could expect during the next few days in the hospital. The very last thing the doctor said to me was, "You should go see your son, he's not expected to live the next 48 hours". My son's father came into the room and we went to see our baby boy. He was connected to so many tubes. My baby boy had on the cutest little shades because the light was too much for him to handle. My heart begins to break. I was not in a good mental place. My son was lying in the incubator and I couldn't even touch him. Because of his premature birth, his skin wasn't developed, so touching him would have been painful. After my boyfriend and I sat there for some time looking, scared, unsure and helpless, we left the NICU and went back to my room. As soon as we got back to my room, my son's father left.

What just happened? The one person that I needed, just abandoned me at my most vulnerable moment. I almost lost my life in an attempt to bring life to our child. Even with the news about our child's life expectancy, you still choose to leave? That night was extremely hard for me. I was exhausted on every level: emotionally, mentally, and physically. I had just become a new mother. My baby was in the NICU fighting for his life. My relationship was a wreck and I had no idea what to expect next. Honestly speaking, I didn't have any expectations other than the norm that was already created. Without any reservation, I ventured back to the NICU to be with my son. If anything was going to happen, I was going to be right there by his side. Always.

MY THOUGHTS

CHAPTER 5
GROUND ZERO

What are your thoughts when you hear the term "Ground Zero?" Most people think about the worldwide tragedy and deaths from September 11th and the World Trade Center. From the impact of the planes to the collapse of the buildings, there was an overbearing release of smoke, fire, trash, debris, and rubbish. Even in this catastrophic event, there is a settling. What do you see when the smoke clears? There would be unassigned and misappropriated pieces everywhere. The foundation of buildings that once reached to the sky would be out of sort. Nothing would be as you previously expected. Well, that was my life – Ground Zero.

When leaving the hospital, all I had were pieces of a life I formerly knew. I had no home, no car, no job and a baby that was fighting to remain alive. I had become a stranger to a place I once called home. I was no longer welcomed. For the first time in my life, I was homeless. I bounced around between the homes of my grandmother, my aunt or the hospital. All I had at this point was my son. He needed me. He depended on me. At a moment's notice. I would get up and head straight to the hospital. I would sit there all day. In some cases, I was made to leave. The verbal and emotional abuse got worse. Even in his absence, the man that I conceived life with taunted, bullied manipulated and controlled me. I completely lost my identity. I hated looking at myself in the mirror. As crazy as this may sound, I was still in love with my abuser. I wanted his attention. I wanted his affection. I wanted him present. This was the personification of manipulative abuse in so many ways. He's the father of my son and I was willing to do anything to give my baby the life that I thought he deserved. The more I allowed, the more he dished out.

Now, here I am as a new mother with no self-esteem, no confidence, no self-worth, and no value. Essentially, I felt like nothing. Of course my family was there but that isn't the same. In my family environment, I was constantly reminded of what I should have done, what I should be doing, and how I should be doing it. The advice offered was based on what they wouldn't put up with and how they think you should feel.

ADVICE:
When a person you love is going through something, be supportive without adding stress. Stress only makes it worse.

Most of the time when advice was offered, I said nothing, but on the inside, I suffered in silence. Nights were sleepless. Days were draining. Stress had completely taken over. Much like the place where the World Trade Center once stood tall, I had officially reached my personal ground zero. At this point in my life, suicide seemed to be an easier task than the life I was currently experiencing.

During the hospital stay, it appeared that my son had become somewhat of a spectacle. The nurses called to inform me that my child's father had too many visitors at the hospital during times where rest was needed for the child. I made his family aware and the arguments started. He was furious because he felt like the nurses were keeping tabs on him and spying on him. The policies and procedures that were in place to keep our baby safe and secure fell on deaf ears. As an act of rebellion, he stopped coming to the hospital altogether. He intentionally missed surgeries and major milestones during our son's progression in the NICU. It was a normal day for me to sit at the hospital while my son's monitor signals for doctors and nurses to rush in for emergency procedures because my son stopped breathing and started to turn blue. As numb as I was emotionally, this was one of the worst feelings ever. I called his dad and he was nowhere to be found.

We were reaching the end of our journey in the NICU and now it was time to go to a transitional room. I hadn't heard from his dad. I wanted to let him know that our bundle of joy would be coming home. Did you catch that?! My miracle baby was coming home!! After multiple life threatening events and being told to not get attached, he's preparing to come home. GOD IS GOOD! Because he was born premature, I had to successfully complete some parenting training programs. Here I go again! As bad as my situation was, I still wanted my son's father to be included in the process so I called him. Surprisingly, he showed up with gifts in hand. Things were great for the first couple of days. We were getting along and functioning as a family. Life was good but, I was reminded of and experienced the old adage, "too good to be true". When his phone rang, he left because evidently, his friends meant more than his newborn son. My baby could be released at any time and I must have a place to live. While putting in applications for an apartment, I was also looking for a car. From somewhere, I pulled strength and the need to motivate myself through this process. After 109 days in the NICU, my baby got a release date to come home, but where is home? In that moment of questioning God, my phone was responding with the answer in the form of not one, but two approvals for apartments. You're Approved! What a breath of fresh air. There was a sense of joy and peace that I didn't know existed. Things were coming together for me…… again. I decided to share my good news with my son's father. I figured he would be happy for me. And he was! He was so supportive. He helped me get things for my apartment and showed interest in his son. He even picked us up from the hospital. I was reminded as to why I loved this man so much. I really believed that <u>this</u> time, things would be different. We wouldn't be in the hospital so why not give it a fair chance? And that's when the broken promises returned.

MY THOUGHTS

_____
_____
_____
_____
_____
_____
_____
_____
_____
_____
_____
_____
_____
_____
_____
_____
_____
_____
_____
_____
_____
_____
_____
_____

CHAPTER 6
BROKEN PROMISES

broke *(past tense of break)*
(verb) – violate or transgress; to invalidate

promise
(noun) - declaration or assurance that one will do a particular thing or that a particular thing will happen

Be not deceived; God is not mocked: for whatsoever a man soweth, that shall he also reap. **Galatians 6:7 (KJV)**

You're approved!! This was by far the best news I had received in quite some time. Two approvals and a release date for my son. Life had finally started coming together. I was beyond excited. Nothing could rob me of this moment, or so I thought. I called my son's father to share with him the good news. For the first time in a long time, he appeared to be happy for me. We went out to celebrate our major accomplishments. Dinner was amazing. The conversation was normal and I was finally in a good space. Then out of nowhere, he reminded of his ability to break promises. He advised me to get the apartment closer to him so he could be more involved with our child. He promised that he would move out of his place and move in with me because he wanted to make things work. He sounded so convincing when he mentioned that our son needed the both of us and I agreed. This was an amazing plan! This was the man I loved! Finally, he wanted what I wanted. Have you ever heard of being blinded by love? Because of this faulty concept, I accepted the apartment close to him.

While we prepared for our new place and our son's release date, the Neonatal Intensive Care Unit (NICU) informed me that our son would me moved to a transition room. The transition room is where the parent assumes fully responsibility for the care of their baby. It's the final step before your baby is released to come home. During our stay in the transition room, my son's father and I decided to get back together. While I was at the hospital during the day, he was at the apartment making sure everything got moved in and that everything was prepared for our son's arrival at his new home. At night, he would come back to the hospital allowing me to rest. I was in love all over again. I couldn't believe it! My son's father was actually doing his part. Present and accounted for. I couldn't begin to describe the feeling. The past few days together as a family were amazing. I believed in his every word. His tone, his words, his behavior and his actions were totally different. He was very convincing.
The day had finally come, after 109 days in the NICU, for us to go home. As a first-time mother, I had so many emotions about going home however, ready or not, the day was here. I called my son's

father to let him know we were ready to come home and he was a no show. The life I thought was a thing of the past, was returning without permission. I was about to fall victim to another level of ignored calls and blatant disrespect. My phone calls went unanswered in volumes. I thoughtfully considered his well-being and that surely something happened in order for him to leave us stranded at the hospital. So, I sat and waited patiently. My phone finally rings, but it is my sister. She saw my boyfriend, but he wasn't alone. He was with his other female friend and her son....... having lunch. For a moment, my heart stopped. Returned feelings of embarrassment and humiliation encompassed me. How did I get back to this position? New baby. New home. No father. This is not how I pictured things. This was not my picture perfect representation. I had to pull myself together. Not for me, but for the little boy who now depends on me solely. My face showed one thing, but you would never know because of the mask I wore on the outside.

MY THOUGHTS

_____
_____
_____
_____
_____
_____
_____
_____
_____
_____
_____
_____
_____
_____
_____
_____
_____
_____
_____
_____
_____
_____
_____
_____
_____

CHAPTER 7
THE MASQUERADE

mas-quer-ade
(verb) - *to dress in costume, to wear a disguise; to conceal*

Paul Laurence Dunbar penned a poetic synopsis of my stage in life in his heroic account of *"We Wear The Mask"*. This poem specifically addresses the position of many people that have to wear a mask of façade to cover scars, wounds, dissatisfaction and disappointment. In my case, you can add embarrassment, humiliation, betrayal and multiple feats of deceit. How often do we go through life wearing these masks? How long must the mask be worn in an attempt to act as if we are ok, when we are not? These non-medical and in most cases, figurative masks show the complete opposite expression of a person that is literally dying on the inside. Well, that had become my new normal. I was living a life of lies. I protected the actions of my son's father even though they weren't in the favor of me or my son. I was crying loud internally and suffering in silence. And this is the clincher. My mask painted a picture wherein no one had a clue. I was functioning day to day, but not living. I was the epitome of the "great pretender". One would think that fulfillment in life would be the result of a new apartment, a new car, and a new baby boy. However, the feeling of being alone weighed heavy on me. In my reactionary measure to respond, nothing I did was right. I still wanted the attention of my son's father. I called his phone multiple times and rode past his house through the day. All of this was against how I normally conducted myself in a relationship. I personified the "gung ho" philosophy. Nothing else mattered. After a couple of months of this insane approach, I came to the realization that what I wanted was not in the best interests of me and my baby. I actually tricked myself into thinking that I was done with it all. I thought I let it go, but slowly and surely, my son's father came back. In a state of hindsight confusion, I welcomed him with open arms.

Sunday after Sunday, I was going to church, singing in the choir, dancing with the praise team and worshipping, but on the inside, I was mentally and spiritually dead. I would smile, hangout, and attend gatherings as normal. Meanwhile, I was suffering at the hands of my abuser. Church was my outlet. It was one of the few places I was allowed to go. I would sit in service questioning God, "why me", "how did I get here" and "why can't I free myself from this". Clearly, I heard God's response when He said, "trust me". Sundays always presented intense fights with me and my boyfriend. This soul tie had completely taken over my life and I didn't have the strength to encourage or pray for myself. I wanted help so bad, but I chose to remain silent and fearful of what people would say.

ADVICE:
LISTEN TO HEAR, NOT TO RESPOND.

For some odd reason, people aren't always supportive of women when it comes to abuse. Some people are quick to judge and say what they would or would not accept but it's not that simple for the one who is directly involved. Let me give you an example. Due to multiple fights that were sparked due to the exchange of our child, my son's father and I decided that we would meet in public areas. One day, he didn't take our son to Head Start so we agreed to meet at the Verizon Wireless store. The exchange started off good until I said something that he didn't like. Apparently, speaking my truths and things that mattered to me was a problem. As I was getting the car seat out of his car, I accidentally hit him with the car seat. With my 2-year-old son standing nearby and in plain sight, he punched me directly in the face. The punch was so hard, it knocked me off my feet and I hit the ground. To add insult to injury, he simply left me on the ground with onlookers that did nothing to help me. These people were unbothered by seeing an individual, a female, get physically assaulted. In another fragile and humiliated state, I got up off the ground to go in the store where I asked the rep to call 911. I was so embarrassed. My secret was out and due to the severity of the blow, I had to take off my mask and come clean with my family.

As I was transported to the hospital, with my baby in my lap, tears and blood filled the onset of my swollen eyes. All I could see was this little person looking up at me with unbiased hope. My only response was "I'm sorry". When my dad walked into the emergency room, I lost it. Have you ever seen a woman cry to the point where all of their successfully placed makeup runs down their entire face? This is how I looked. It wasn't makeup, but the mask that I wore for years to prove my case to a premeditated jury was off. There was no turning back. Excuses were non-existent. I had no other choice but to tell my family, my truths.

MY THOUGHTS

_____
_____
_____
_____
_____
_____
_____
_____
_____
_____
_____
_____
_____
_____
_____
_____
_____
_____
_____
_____
_____
_____
_____
_____
_____
_____
_____

CHAPTER 8
THE LAST STRAW

After being discharged from the hospital for a fractured socket and torn ligaments in my left eye, I had to turn myself in for a warrant where I was assaulted. You read that correctly. Yes! I was arrested. While I was at the hospital with injuries, he went downtown to the magistrate's office and had a warrant issued for assault. I had to be processed as a criminal with a mugshot that will forever be documented on my personal file and record with a black eye. My life was never the same. Then, the questions came from family, friends, and the general public. Everyone had questions but no one offered solutions.

For the next month, my son and I lived with my parents. Out of fear, I had to be monitored. My dysfunctional relationship had become functional for me. My abnormal connection with a person that abused me on so many levels had become my new norm. Being away from him didn't seem right to me. I wanted his attention. As time went on, we started texting. He apologized for what was done and dropped the charges against me. What started as sneaky rendezvous, became a self-proclaimed exodus from my parent's house back to the home, environment and atmosphere that had become a toxic cycle.

I knew I didn't want to live my life in fear, but it was all I knew from a fearfully comfortable place and that made it hard for me to leave. One day, I was riding in the car and John P. Kee's song, "Life and Favor" was playing. I remember saying to GOD, "I have to get out of this". As normal, He responded, but with a negative resolve. He said, "If you go back, he'll kill you". That should have been the final verdict, game, set and match for this naïve mind. This relationship was like a drug to me. I knew it was bad for me but I just couldn't walk away.

Here's the result of an addictive drug/relationship. We planned to have family dinner one day. He told me to meet him at his house at 6:00pm. When I get there, there was a car in the driveway that I didn't recognize. My son was already in the house per our schedule. I walk in the house with full access as normal. He's in there having sex while my child is sleep in the same room. I snapped! I went into the living room looking for something. I have no idea what, but just something. By the time I returned to the hallway headed to that bedroom, my son's father and his lover were coming towards me. We exchanged words and she proceeds to throw a picture, ironically of my son and I, at me. The frame cuts my lip. As I head towards her to retaliate, he grabs me and takes me outside. In the driveway, we yell and scuffle right before he purposefully head butts me. Boom! I fall to the ground and I don't remember much after that. Once I came to myself, I realized not only had he left me for dead but my child was in the car. While to this day I'm still uncertain of how long I laid there, I got up and drove home. That drive was the longest 20 minutes of my life. When I got home in route to my door, my neighbor screamed out. I looked at her like she had lost her mind not knowing that it was me that was actually losing it. She grabbed my son and helped me into her apartment. She made me aware that my forehead was open. I had braids and she helped me take my braids out. I can remember all the blood in my hair. I was on the ground for so long that my braids were completely saturated in blood. I mean you could literally squeeze the braid and the blood would pour to the floor. I drove myself to the hospital. In the car, I had another conversation with God. This was a prayer that I'm sure God had heard on many occasions. "God, if I can just make it back home to my son, I promise I'll never go back". Two more torn ligaments in my left eye and 22 stitches later, I said no more. This was definitely the last straw. I couldn't take it anymore. As I'm getting stitched up, he calls. He plays the same record that I've heard so many times before.

Track One: *He Apologized*
Track Two: *He Didn't Mean It*
Bonus Track: *Had I Listened To Him, This Would've Never Happened*

Was he serious? Had I listened? So, this was my fault. As I sat on the phone with him, I started questioning myself. Was this my fault? I knew it wasn't but, he had this clever and crazy way of passing the blame without accepting responsibility for his own actions. The end of that phone call was the end of us. There was a moment when I looked in the mirror and could not recognize the woman I had become. I didn't know the person that was looking back at me. She was a stranger. Was I even capable of being loved? Who would love me knowing all that I endured?

As time progressed, I met a guy from New York. Dating and trusting another man was not in my skeptical mind. I was fresh out of an abusive relationship. He complimented the beauty in the stitches in the middle of my forehead. He was very persistent. He helped uplift me and show me why I deserved to be loved. He introduced me to what it felt like to be loved, the right way. The attention he gave me was different, unfamiliar and something I hadn't felt in quite some time. I decided to give love a try one more chance.

MY THOUGHTS

_____
_____
_____
_____
_____
_____
_____
_____
_____
_____
_____
_____
_____
_____
_____
_____
_____
_____
_____
_____
_____
_____

CHAPTER 9
THE REPEATED CYCLE

re-peat
(verb) - *to cause to happen again, to duplicate*

Abuse doesn't begin and end with just physical contact. You have mental, emotional and verbal abuse as well. Have you ever heard the saying that you are what you attract? My resolve is that there is some truth to that. Even though I was free from the previous relationship that was physically abusive, I was still trapped mentally. I wasn't sure how to maneuver in my daily life. I still allowed the relationship of my past to control me and how I operated in my new relationship. My complication came in the form of trying to love myself and receive love from a new person. This new guy was like a breath of fresh air. We were hanging out all the time. My son loved him. My family loved him. My friends loved him. He and I had become thick as thieves. I wasn't sure if I could trust him and I didn't know how. He was patient with me and because of that, I let my guard down. He knew how to handle and protect me when my son's father would show up at my apartment or call in an attempt to keep me entangled in his web.

He stood in confidence and it made me feel safe. For the foreseeable future, that's what I needed.

Due to a career change, he decided to attend barber school. He relocated to Charlotte, North Carolina. We embarked upon a long-distance relationship. I soon found out that I was pregnant with my second son. I called to inform him of the good news while I was sitting in the doctor's office. He was super excited but, nervous to tell his family that he was expecting his first child. He relocated from Charlotte, North Carolina to Columbia, South Carolina and that's when the change happened. At the time, he was living with a Pastor and their family. For some time, he would have to sneak to call me and then the lines of communication went blank. He would no longer accept my calls and if he did call, he was rude. I decided to focus more on the fact that I was now about to be the mother of not 1, but 2 children.

During one of the doctor visits, I learned that my baby had Mosaic Turner Syndrome. It's a genetics' disorder that comes with tons of health issues. I was devastated. I knew nothing about caring for a child with a disability. I did my best to keep my son's father abreast of all updates from the doctor's office. One day, I called him to give him an update and to my surprise, he no longer claimed to be the father of the child I was carrying. From that point, I was bullied. I gave birth to my 2nd child on March 17, 2007, which was early at 29 weeks. Once again, I reached out to him to let him that our son was here. He passed the phone to the wife of the Pastor that he was living with and by her, I was told that he will not be doing anything for that baby until we have a paternity test. I was also told that only upon successful proof will he do his part as the father. Lastly, I was told to never contact him again. I was crushed. Is this the same man who said he would always protect me?

After 35 days in the Neonatal Intensive Care Unit (NICU), a facility that I knew very well, I received a phone call from my son's father telling me that he and his Pastor's wife were on the way to Asheville to see Isaiah. For it to be his first encounter with his son, it was very awkward. I felt like I was being watched and like I was being interrogated. I asked him if he wanted to sign the birth certificate. She immediately answered, "not until we have the DNA test results". I didn't understand why she included herself in the "we" of that response. I didn't know her and vice versa. He didn't sign the birth certificate. Upon leaving the hospital, she said, "I'll be in touch with you regarding the details of the DNA test" and they both departed. After receiving the expected results of the DNA test, I never received an apology and things got worse.

After 45 days in the NICU, my new son and I were going home. My family of 2 was now a family of 3. I called my son's father as normal, to let him know that we were home and he was free to come visit. He did just that, but not alone. He came to visit accompanied by the Pastor's wife and another church member. I felt like a visitor in my own home. We weren't allowed to have private conversations concerning our son. I had to be observed as if I couldn't be trusted in my own home. I'm sure that the perceptions of the Pastor's wife concerning me were fueled by lies and manipulation. I harbored such hate for her. I know that's a strong word but I didn't know that a Pastor's wife could be so judgmental and mean. Even with the treatment from her towards me for something that I didn't do, my son's father never apologized for her actions. He just stepped into a role that was never questioned and acted as if things were normal. He was good for playing mind games. He knew that I wasn't mentally strong and he used that to his advantage. He knew that I wanted a family and he used me. He would call me for money. I had to pay bills. I co-signed for him to get a house. I even moved to Columbia. I wasn't allowed to mention where I was or tag him on social media because he didn't want the people at the church to know that we were living together. When his Pastor found out, he conjured a lie that I was homeless and needed a place to stay. We could never ride to church together. Everything we did was a secret just to help him maintain his image at the church. I stayed with him while he entertained the company of numerous women. He told me that they were just his friends, but he was sleeping with them. I was trapped in the same vicious cycle and didn't know how to get out. There were times when I knew something wasn't right, but he would make me believe I was crazy.

On Valentine's Day, we went to dinner. He made me aware that he had a baby on the way, but he didn't want me to leave. He had been in a relationship with one of the members of the church. At one point, he was dating multiple women at the same church and I had no idea. After the news of the pregnancy, I decided to leave. This was not an easy task. He called the police on me for trying to get my items out of the house. This was the same house that I co-signed for and the same house that we shared. After that, I was done. His lies weighed heavy on me and once again, suicide felt easier than having to deal with this torment and humiliation. My life was saved because of my kids. They needed me so I moved on. Having a special needs child came with a lot of responsibilities and requirements. Peace, patience and perseverance were some of those daily requirements. Imagine sitting in the waiting room as your son goes through surgery. Now, imagine that same ordeal, in the same waiting room with your son's father and his new lover. As much as I tried to exercise patience, I was naively vulnerable as he explained to me that the female was his co-worker. He knew that I still loved him, but he retreated to continue in a position of control and manipulation. I couldn't take it anymore. Enough was enough. It was time I got back to me - the real me. The me minus the hurt and heartache. Before I could offer myself to anyone else, I had to deal with myself and come to the conclusion that I deserved more and deserved better than what was being offered to me. I had to break free of the vicious cycles and toxic relationships that were my excepted norm. By any means necessary, I made the decision to make a turn for the better. I needed a clean slate and the process began.

MY THOUGHTS

CHAPTER 10
NEW BEGINNINGS

strength
(noun) - *power, endurance*

new
(adjective) - *not having been seen or used*

be-gin-ning
(noun) - *the start of something*

Domestic violence and its multiplicity of forms come in repeated cycles if not properly monitored. These cycles, as the exact definition explain, can manifest from one relationship to another if not acknowledged and dealt with in confidence. I had come to the conclusion that I had enough. I had to own myself mentally, physically and emotionally. That meant maintaining my future and expectancy with a firm grip. Physically, the straw that broke the camel's back was when I was hit and left for dead on the ground. Emotionally and mentally, I had to make the decision to protect my sanity and ultimately my children without compromise.

So, I made the decision to begin anew. It was time I get back to me. What did that look like? Where do I start? The first thing I had to do was be honest with myself. I had to have a serious heart to heart with my biggest critic, Me. I had to own the role I played in the relationship, forget about what I knew about myself and remember what I deserved. There were many times I had fallen and considered going back. Secondly, I had to change my mindset. Internally, I had to change the way that I thought about myself and the ways that I dealt with my personal struggles. I spent some time alone to simply get to know myself. I went on dates with myself. I took myself to dinner and a movie. In that, I rediscovered my inner beauty even if there were flaws. I had to encourage and motivate myself. I didn't allow myself to just say things. I had to put them into action.

For many, it may seem to be minor, but I even had to stop receiving phone calls from my son's father. I protected my environment at all costs. Some of these costs were breaking cycles and ridding myself of communications that would absorb me into defeated positions. Then, those costs would come with personal rewards. If I could make it through a full day without being belittled or negated in some form or fashion, I deserved to celebrate myself. You must realize that repeated behaviors become habits. One day at a time, I was able to create a more positive environment that encompassed mental, emotional and physical stability. Once this space and environment was created, I noticed that I was becoming a better version of myself which included me becoming a better mother.

My new life includes work, school, church and my honorable responsibility, motherhood. I never miss a school activity or sporting event. I push my boys and love on them. When I neglected myself, they suffered. As a parent, I never want to be the reason for my children to need counseling. You must be mindful of the things you say and do around your children while wounded. Lift up your kids. As you motivate yourself, motivate them. Encourage them as you encourage yourself. Your children need your support and more importantly, they need your prayers: with and for them. I'm attentive to their needs. My kids are my strength and my motivating why.

How did I make it out? How did I make it here? It's only by the grace of God and my daily affirmations. Daily, I had to maintain a consistency of positive reinforcements which include prayer and positive affirmations. My most memorable affirmation was "I am not who they say I am, but I am who GOD says I am". If you don't heal within, you will always attract what's in you. When I started dating again, I was guarded more securely than Fort Knox. I was guarded and they were living. The wall that I built to protect myself was also holding me hostage. I experienced true freedom when I applied the scripture that declares, *"if the son sets you free, you will be free indeed"*. **(John 8:36 NIV)** I was free to love again. I was free to trust again. I was free to be me. It's because of that same freedom that I am here and I'm able to encourage you and motivate you.

YOU CAN DO THIS!!!

It may seem to be the hardest thing for you to accomplish, but trust me, over time, it gets easier. Let me be the first to celebrate your first accomplishment. I'm sure you're wondering what I am celebrating? By reading this book and all the trial by error circumstances that I had to overcome, you've made a decision. I want to commend you for choosing you. Why does choosing yourself seem like the wrong choice? I'm so glad you asked. When you realize that loving him is breaking and altering you as an individual, that's a clear indication of two uncertainties. First, you have to consider yourself and your well- being. Secondly, it's time to go. Oftentimes, we consider the feelings of others more than our own feelings. Sometimes, that includes the feelings of the abuser. As progressively as we think, it is common to hear women say "he does it because he loves me". These same women accept misappropriated blame by saying, "it was me" and "maybe I shouldn't have done that."

Hear this - love doesn't hurt. According to **1 Corinthians 13:4-7 (NIV)**, *"Love is patient, love is kind. It does not envy, it does not boast, it is not proud. It does not dishonor others, it is not self-seeking, it is not easily angered, it keeps no record of wrongs. Love does not delight in evil but rejoices with the truth. It always protects, always trusts, always hopes, always perseveres."* Please remember, GOD is LOVE! Take your voice back! Start looking in the mirror and acknowledging the woman looking back at you. Once upon a time, she was once broken but I am here to help you and push you to the original plan. Here are a few things that I did to regain self-worth and self-love. The key word in both of those words is SELF. Essentially, this must start with you.

Most buildings that are frequented with mass gatherings have an escape plan. These escape plans dictate the best method to get from where you are in the building to a safe place. During natural disasters, city and state officials implement an escape plan for the citizens to get away from possible dangers to safe havens.

MARQUITA'S ESCAPE PLAN

There hath no temptation taken you but such as is common to man: but God is faithful, who will not suffer you to be tempted above that ye are able; but will with the temptation also make a way to escape, that ye may be able to bear it.
1 Corinthians 10:13 KJV

1. Prayer Life
2. Watch Your Words
3. Thought Process
4. Forgiveness
5. Trust

Let me introduce you to Marquita's Escape Plan. There are five tools and concepts that created a way of escape for me when dealing with domestic violence and they remain constant in my life to this very day. The five tools/concepts are prayer, the use of my words, how I think, forgiveness and trust.

Without prayer, I would be lost. My relationship with God was never compromised or forsaken. I may have made some bad decisions, but I maintained a direct connection to God through prayer. I believe that according to **Acts 17:28**, *"it is in Him that I live, move and had my being"*. I believe that according to **Philippians 4:13** that *"I can do all things through Christ which strengtheneth me"*. Prayer is my foundation and not just a major factor, but the deciding factor in my life. It kept me from taking my own life and continues to keep me sane. The immediate response from God through prayer made me comparable to Nike. I had no time to waste. I had to "Just Do It!" There was no more stalling or procrastinating. Even though family was around, I had to make some boss moves on my own. I couldn't depend on anyone else. I chose to speak life into myself. You can do the same thing.

The word of God tells us that life and death are in the power of the tongue **(Proverbs 18:21)**. That leads me to my next point. You must be mindful of what you are speaking. When you aren't feeling your best, remember, "You are snared by the words of your mouth" **(Proverbs 6:2)**.

Decree and Declare:
I AM CREATED IN GOD'S IMAGE.
I AM AN INTELLIGENT VIRTUOUS WOMAN.
I AM WHO GOD SAYS I AM.

Next, you must change your thought process. Forget what you know about you. Forget what others may know about you. Focus on what GOD thinks. The scripture tells us in Proverbs **23:7** *"As a man thinketh in his heart, so is he"*. You become what you think. If you think success, you'll be successful. If you think failure, you will definitely fail. Make sure that you guard your thoughts. Stop having self-defeating thoughts. Stop counting yourself out before you even get started. If you can make one step, you can make another one. Make those successful steps the new cycle. The enemy will always remind you of your past. He will cause you to think that you will never be more or better than your current situation. Being alone, can cause you to think about numerous encounters of abuse. You have the power to send those thoughts back to sender. If you don't command your thoughts, you will setup yourself up for unnecessary warfare. Guard your mind at all cost.

Decree and Declare:

I AM AN OVERCOMER.

I AM MORE THAN ENOUGH.

I HAVE WHAT IT TAKES TO WIN.

Next, you have to forgive yourself .... and your abuser. Readily, we position ourselves to do the first part, but rarely have we considered the second part. If you, don't forgive with your whole heart, you will remain enslaved. The individual and situation will always control you and that's not what you want to happen. Forgiveness isn't for them. It's for you. When you forgive, that doesn't mean that you have forgotten the situation. It just means that you refuse to allow the situation to control you. When you hold on to things, it becomes your owner. If you choose to hold on to unforgiveness, it'll cause you to become bitter, angry, and will cause added stress. Stress is a silent killer. You must forgive to be free. I believe that forgiving yourself is more rewarding than actually forgiving your abuser. You may look at forgiveness of yourself and your abuser as a hard thing. You can do it!

Lastly, you must learn to trust again. Everyone isn't out to get you. While this step along with the others may take some time, know that GOD has someone in mind concerning you. Once you have been violated by someone that says that they love you the most, it's hard to think that they're not all the same. Once you have forgiven your abuser and yourself, free yourself. You are no longer the woman you once were. You don't accept or respond to things as you have previously. Be willing and understanding that you are not alone and that many women have suffered with this. Show yourself some compassion. Be patient and allow yourself room to grow. You might make mistakes, but that's life and you are not perfect. Take what you have gone and grown through as learning experiences. Give yourself permission and time to heal.

Remember, it all begins with you and you must get to a place of wholeness.

While moving forward in life, trust the process. It'll take time for you to get out of the vicious cycle of repetitious behaviors such as apologizing, attempting to right a wrong, or feeling like you are not being enough. YOU ARE MORE THAN ENOUGH. You have to make the decision to live. How do you do that? Show up for yourself every day. Be your own spokesperson every day. Make a decision on what and who you want to be and then go and be that person. The only way you can remain in a posture of strength is to maintain a consistent prayer life. Don't just speak what you want to happen. Believe that what you are asking for will happen.

I wanted to share my story so you would understand that you are not alone. Seek help. You don't have to suffer in silence. Recognize your potential. You are capable of doing whatever you put your mind to. Set daily goals for yourself. Start small and then work yourself up. Celebrate every achievement! I am a living testament of how, with the help of the Lord, you can make it out of any negative situation. You don't have to submit to situations that aren't in your favor or to your advantage. Life is a journey filled with transitions, trials and triumphs. If I can get out, so can you! If I can live a life of love, you can too! More than anything, you don't have to settle for mediocrity.

YOU CAN SUCCESSFULLY LIVE A LIFE
THAT MOVES
FROM STRUGGLE TO STRENGTH!

MY THOUGHTS

_____
_____
_____
_____
_____
_____
_____
_____
_____
_____
_____
_____
_____
_____
_____
_____
_____
_____
_____
_____
_____
_____
_____
_____
_____
_____
_____

SCRIPTURES TO HELP ALONG THE WAY

Ezekiel 36:26 (NIV)

I will give you a new heart and put a new spirit in you; I will remove from you your heart of stone and give you a heart of flesh.

Philippians 4:13 (NIV)

I can do all this through him who gives me strength.

Proverbs 3:5-6 (NIV)

Trust in the LORD with all your heart and lean not on your own understanding; in all your ways submit to him, and he will make your paths straight.

Psalms 139:13-14 (NIV)

For you created my inmost being; you knit me together in my mother's womb. I praise you because I am fearfully and wonderfully made; your works are wonderful, I know that full well.

Domestic Violence Resources

In The Event Of An Emergency, Please Dial 911

Local Shelters and Hotlines
National Domestic Violence Hotline
800-799-7233
Or Text **LOVEIS** To 22522

The Abigail Project (Columbia, SC)   Sistercare (Cayce, SC)
803-931-2246   803-765-9428

Safe Passage (Rock Hill, SC)   Safe Harbor (Greenville, SC)
803-329-3336   800-291-2139

Helpmate (Asheville, NC)   Warring Angels (Asheville, NC)
828-254-0516   828-253-2968

S.C. Coalition Against Domestic Violence (Columbia, SC)
803-256-2900

CASA Family Services (Orangeburg, SC)
803-534-2272

Meg's House (Greenwood, SC)
888-847-3915

Origin Family Violence (Charleston, SC)
843-735-7802

New Direction of Horry County (Myrtle Beach, SC)
843-945-4902

CYCLES OF DOMESTIC VIOLENCE

1. Abuse
Partner lashes out with aggressive, belittling or violent behavior

2. Guilt
After, your partner feels guilt, but not over what he's done, more so of being caught and facing consequences for his abusive behavior.

3. Excuses
Rationalizes what he or she has done. They blame you for the abusive behavior.

4. Normal Behavior
Does everything to regain control and keep victim in the relationship. He may act as if nothing happened, turn on the charm, put on the charm, put on the honeymoon phase to make the victim believe he's changed.

5. Fantasy and Planning

Abuser begins to fantasize about abusing you again. He spends a lot of time thinking about what you did wrong. He then turns the fantasy into reality.

6. Set-up
Your abuser sets you up and puts his plan in motion, creating a situation where he can justify abusing you.

SIGNS OF DOMESTIC VIOLENCE

1. You are frightened by your partner's temper
2. You are afraid to disagree with your partner
3. You have been kicked or shoved by your partner
4. You don't see your family or friends
5. You have been forced to have sex or afraid to say no to sex
6. You are forced to explain everything you do, everywhere you go, every person you see to avoid your partner's temper.
7. You spend more and more of your time making promises, apologizing, and living in guilt and fear.

TYPES OF ABUSE

1. Physical
2. Emotional
3. Verbal
4. Financial
5. Sexual
6. Mental

TACTICS USED TO MANIPULATE

1. Dominance
2. Humiliation
3. Isolation
4. Threats
5. Intimidation
6. Denial and Blame

CREDIT

Holy Bible
New International Version

Holy Bible
New King James Version

Holy Bible
King James Version

Paul Laurence. Dunbar, ""We Wear the Mask."" from The
Complete Poems of Paul Laurence Dunbar. (New York: Dodd,
Mead and Company)

John P. Kee
"Life and Favor" (2012)

Cover Graphics By
TB VISUALS

Marquita Nesbitt's Attire By
LUXE BY TREVON LUTHER

Hair and Makeup By
THE ULTIMATE REMEDY BY ARIEL SYMONE

Photography By
RHYAN HILLS CINESHOTS

Edited By
RED PEN EDITS AND CONSULTING, LLC

ABOUT MARQUITA NESBITT

Marquita Nesbitt is a new author and successful mother from Asheville, North Carolina. She currently lives in Columbia, South Carolina with her two sons, Kenneth and Isaiah. She is a Domestic Violence Survivor. She received her Certification as a Nursing Assistant and later received her Certification in Medical Office Administration. Her favorite hobby is to color. SHE LOVES TO COLOR!

Marquita is an active member of the All Nations Church of God In Christ (Columbia, SC) under the leadership of Superintendent Nate' M. Jefferson and Lady Tarsha Jefferson. She serves in the Helps and Hospitality Departments. Marquita is also a member of the Church of God In Christ's South Carolina Jurisdiction Evangelism Department where she assists Evangelist Deborah White with the Abigail Project, an initiative to provide resources and tools for domestic violence issues.

Marquita has two favorite scriptures:
Jeremiah 29:11 (KJV) *"For I know the thoughts I think towards you says the Lord, thoughts of peace and not evil, to give you a future and hope."*
and
Psalms 46:1 (KJV) *"God is our refuge and strength, a very present help in trouble."*
Her reason for writing this missive is based on her experience with domestic violence and her advocacy work to help other women escape from that type of life and live in a world of intentional fulfillment. This is her first novel and she hopes that it creates positive trends of women's empowerment.

Made in the USA
Columbia, SC
03 May 2024

34864027R00039